Give Thanks

Karla Dornacher

THOMAS NELSON
Since 1798

Designed by Karla Dornacher
Project Manager: Lisa Stilwell

ISBN: 978-1-4041-8753-5

Printed and bound in China
09 10 11 12 [HH] 6 5 4 3 2 1

Dear Friend,

Giving thanks to God is a good thing, and we have so many things to be thankful for, don't we? The list is truly endless.

And yet so often, just like you, I can get side tracked by the fast pace of everyday life or bogged down by the struggles I face, that I forget to stop and give thanks to God who has blessed me beyond measure. I have learned, however, that having a grateful heart is a choice we make despite our circumstances. Sometimes we just need a little prompting and encouragement to turn our eyes away from what is wrong with life and, instead look to the Giver of life, His goodness, and His grace.

This little book, I pray, will be just the encouragement you need to stir your heart to count your blessings...maybe even see some that you've never thought of before...and give God thanks!! May the Lord bless you as you do!

In His love and for His glory,
Karla

In everything

give thanks

for this is
the will of God
in Christ Jesus
for you.

1 Thessalonians 5:18

From the rising of the sun to its going down,
the Lord's name is to be praised.

Psalm 113:3

There is no schedule when it comes to giving thanks to God.
You can thank Him in the morning when you pray to start your day.
You can set your alarm to remind yourself to give Him thanks at lunchtime.
And bedtime offers the opportunity to reflect on...and give thanks for...
the blessings you might have taken for granted throughout the day.

But what about all those other minutes of the day?
That moment when you looked out the window and saw the sunrise
and the breathtaking beauty of the Lord filling the skies?
Do you have to wait until noon to thank Him for this glorious display?
Of course not!
Or what about when you almost ran into the car that pulled out
in front of you—but you didn't? Should you wait until you go to bed
to thank God for giving you quick reflexes and good brakes?
No way!

Every moment of every day—from the rising of the sun
to the setting of the same—provides us an opportunity to
cultivate a thankful heart.
If you look around you, wherever you are, you'll see a myriad
of earthly blessings to be thankful for...including the sun itself!
You may not have seen it rise, but it did.
And without the sun we could not survive.
God designed it to be the perfect distance from the earth so that it
lights up the darkness, warms up the air, and sustains our lives.

Now that's something to be thankful for!

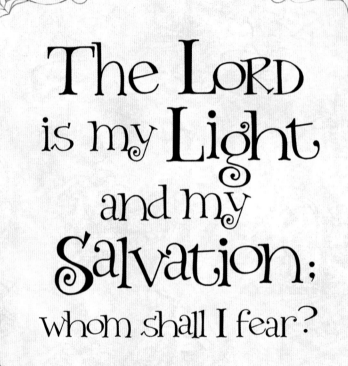

The LORD is my Light and my Salvation; whom shall I fear?

Psalm 27:1

Heavenly Father,

It is incredible to think about how, in the beginning,
there was only darkness but when You spoke, the darkness parted
and the heavens and earth were filled with light!

Thank You, Lord, for creating such heavenly ways
to display Your light:
brilliant sunlight, peaceful moonlight, and twinkling stars.
When I look up and see Your handiwork
I am reminded of Your glory.

I am so grateful God, for all the ways I experience light…
even though most of the time I take it and You for granted.

Not only do I delight in the lights of the sky but I'm also thankful for
the lights that make my house a home:
electric lights, flickering candles, and logs burning in the fireplace.

And thank You Lord for flashlights, headlights, and streetlights
for I can't imagine life without them!

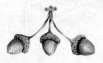

But most of all, I thank You, Father, that You are Light
and that You sent Your Son Jesus to be the Light of this world
and the Light of my life.

Today, Lord, I pray for the Light of Your Word to be my guide
and the Light of Your love to shine brighter than ever
in me and through me for Your glory.

Amen.

I love taking an old piece of furniture and giving it new life by stripping
off the old paint and replacing it with a fresh, clean coat of color.
It makes my heart glad to save something
that was headed for the trash and give it a second chance.

I'm sure if that table could talk, it would say, "Thank you."
I know I would-or would I?
After a few weeks of settling into daily life
and having the compliments dwindle,
would I begin to take my new life for granted?
After receiving a few watermarks from careless glasses
and being used as a resting place for dishes and dirty feet,
would I become discontent with this new life?
Would I forget about my salvation from the trash heap?

Sometimes I'm afraid the routine of everyday life can have that effect on us.
We can forget that God, in His infinite mercy,
has saved us from the trash heap of eternal death and destruction.

The Bible tells us that we are new creations in Christ.
Just as the butterfly looks nothing like the lowly worm it once was,
so it is with us: the old is gone and all things have become new.
But God didn't use sandpaper and paint.
He used the death and resurrection of Jesus. Unconditional love.
Undeserved favor.

Now that's something to be thankful for.

It is good to give thanks to the LORD.

Psalm 92:1

14

When you think about how God has transformed your life,
what are you most thankful for?

Thanksgiving does not come naturally to most of us.
We are much more prone to look at what we don't have
rather than at what we do have...
to see the glass half-empty rather than half-full.
Instead of giving thanks for God's goodness and provision in our lives,
we tend to whine or complain about what's missing or not to our liking.
We also tend to compare our blessings to someone else's, and when we do,
discontentment sneaks in and robs us of the joy of having a grateful heart.

I remember a time when I saw mobile homes as tin cans and swore
I would never live in one. And then the day came when we found ourselves
financially destitute and living in a camper designed for the back of a pickup.
After three months of dwelling in such tiny, cramped quarters,
we were given the opportunity to move into a single-wide trailer.
I was thrilled! My perspective had changed, and I saw that mobile home
as God's provision and my mansion! My heart overflowed with thanksgiving.

God has promised to provide for all of our needs according to His riches in
glory. It pleases God to bless His people. And He does. Just look around you at
your family and friends. The roof over your head. The food in your cupboards.
The talents He's given you. And those are just a few of your earthly blessings.
The list is endless!

When you begin to add your spiritual blessings to the list—salvation, forgiveness,
a personal relationship with Jesus, the indwelling Holy Spirit—
the things you don't have aren't quite as important, are they?

Count your blessings...name them one by one...and give God thanks!

When upon life's billows you are tempest-tossed,
When you are discouraged, thinking all is lost,
Count your many blessings, name them one by one,
And it will surprise you what the Lord hath done.

Count your blessings, name them one by one,
Count your blessings, see what God hath done!
Count your blessings, name them one by one,
And it will surprise you what the Lord hath done.

Are you ever burdened with a load of care?
Does the cross seem heavy you are called to bear?
Count your many blessings, every doubt will fly,
And you will keep singing as the days go by.

When you look at others with their lands and gold,
Think that Christ has promised you His wealth untold;
Count your many blessings—wealth can never buy
Your reward in heaven, nor your home on high.

Count your blessings, name them one by one,
Count your blessings, see what God hath done!
Count your blessings, name them one by one,
And it will surprise you what the Lord hath done.

So, amid the conflict whether great or small,
Do not be disheartened, God is over all;
Count your many blessings, angels will attend,
Help and comfort give you to your journey's end.

—Johnson Oatman, Jr.

Have you ever thought about what an incredible privilege it is for ordinary people,
folks like you and me, to enter into the presence of Almighty God?
Humbling to consider, to say the least.

Almighty God is holy... sinless, perfect, pure.
There's absolutely no dirt hiding in the corners or under the carpet.
We, on the other hand, are sinful, imperfect, and impure
from carrying our sin nature in our hearts and rubbing shoulders with the world.

Yet, because God loves us and longs for relationship with us,
He invites us to come to Him just as we are.
We are not required to clean ourselves up or dust ourselves off.
We are not obligated to attain some of level
of spiritual success or perfection in order to gain access to the King.
We are told simply to enter with thanksgiving.
How can this be?

This invitation is almost inconceivable until you draw near and see the bloodstains
on the gate and remember who went before you to prepare your way.
The gate is open wide, and the crimson stains call out the price that was paid
on the cross so that you could gain entrance into God's throne room.
You can do nothing to earn your entrance or to open the gates any wider.
You can only say yes to God's invitation, accept Christ's payment by faith,
and enter His gates with thanksgiving.

Thank God today for the blood of Jesus,
for it is only by His blood that we are able to enter into His presence.

King of Kings

Psalm 100:4

Enter into His gates with thanksgiving, and into His courts with praise.

Enter into His gates with thanksgiving, and into His courts with praise.

We all talk to ourselves, don't we?
I know I do, and so did David, the psalmist.

One of my favorite psalms is 103,
where, in essence, David does a little self-talk
to help him refocus on the things that matter.

He basically says to himself,
"Now listen to me, my soul.
Despite what's going on in the world,
stop right now and bless the Lord.
Don't forget all He's done for you, soul.
Think about those things and give Him glory!"

David goes on to count his blessings,
naming them one by one.

So next time your soul is downcast, try this:
Tell your soul to take a break from the pain,
to consider the good that is in your life,
and to bless the Lord!

Bless the
LORD
O my soul,
and all that
is within me,

bless

His

holy

Name.

Psalm 103:1

23

But what about the circumstances in my life that are not blessings?
What about my struggles, my grief, my loneliness, my pain, my past?
How can I give thanks for those?

God knows that living in this world is not easy.
He doesn't expect you to deny your problems or pretend all is well when it isn't.
Instead, He longs for you to invite Him into your pain
and then let genuine thanksgiving well up from a heart hidden in Him.

The Lord God is your refuge and strength...your present help in times of trouble.
He is with you always and always faithful to His Word.
As you thank Him for His presence and His promises,
you open your heart to receive His peace...
a supernatural peace that only comes to a heart that's confident in Him.

I remember a time, years ago, when my daughter had walked away from God.
The Lord assured me that her decision for Him had been real and that,
despite what it looked like, Satan could not pluck her out of His hand.
In a conversation one day, she asked me if I was worried about her.
I honestly answered no. Then I explained to her that I only had two choices:
I could either worry about her or pray and trust God to take care of her.
I had chosen to invite God into this painful circumstance in my life.
Trusting Him and His promises brought a confident peace to my soul
and thanksgiving to my lips.

Remember...don't just pray and walk away.
In your times of need, thank God for His presence,
His promises, His power, and His plan.
Then just watch how your thanksgiving will bring you peace and Him glory!

Be anxious for NOTHING,
but in EVERYTHING
by prayer and supplication,
with THANKSGIVING,
let your requests
be made known to God;
and the PEACE OF GOD
which surpasses all understanding,
will guard your hearts and minds
through CHRIST JESUS.

Philippians 4:6

Look at the birds of the air,
for they neither sow nor reap
nor gather into barns;
yet your heavenly Father
feeds them.
Are you not of more value
than they?

Matthew 6:26

Feathered Friends Fruity Feeders

My granddaughters and I had such a fun time making these cute little bird feeders together, I'm sure you will too. They are easy to make, eco-friendly, and a great way to bless the neighborhood birds!

Simply cut an orange in half and scoop out the pulp. Poke three holes evenly spaced around the edge of the orange about an inch from the top so they don't rip through. Thread jute, ribbon, or pipe cleaners through the holes, secure, and gather to form a loop at the top for hanging.

Filling your new fruity feeder with a store-bought wild bird seed mix is the easiest way to please your feathered friends but for variety you can mix and fill with a little batter of peanut butter, bird seed, and your choice of unsweetened cereal, dried fruits, or nuts. Hang from a branch or the eave of your house and enjoy the birds and the fruit of your labor!

What circumstances are you struggling with right now?
Have you invited God into your pain? If so, how has His
presence affected you? If not, will you invite Him in today?

_____

_____

_____

_____

_____

_____

_____

_____

_____

_____

_____

_____

_____

It's so easy to become consumed by our adversities—
by big things...by little things...
and by little things we imagine to be bigger than they really are.
When our focus on God begins to shift, our problems become so much bigger than Him!
Without realizing it, we open the door to hopelessness and begin a downward spiral
into despair. Before long, all we can see is what is wrong with life,
and we become trapped in our negative thoughts and emotions.

Several years ago I found myself in one of those traps and I cried out to God for help.
Once when I was praying, a scripture came to mind, and I knew it was from God.
He said, "Take your thoughts into captivity unto Christ" (2 Corinthians 10:5).
My thoughts were out of control, and I longed to capture them,
but my response was "Lord, I want to, but I don't know how!"

He answered with Philippians 4:8. As I opened my Bible and began to read those words,
I realized that everything I had been thinking about
was the exact opposite of what I found in that passage.

I typed out that verse and made several copies of it. I posted them everywhere.
On the fridge. On the windowsill above the kitchen sink. In the car.
On the wall across from the toilet. On the bathroom mirror.
Every time my eye fell upon that verse, I would check my thoughts
to see if they lined up with the truth of God's Word and the truth of who He is.

Gradually, as my negative thoughts were replaced with God's promises and perspective,
my hope was renewed, and I realized that even if there is nothing good about my
circumstances, God is always good and worthy of my praise and thanksgiving.

Praise and thanksgiving open the door to hope, and hope lifts us up above
our circumstances. Such heavenly hope ushers us into the joy of the Lord.

Whatever is true,
whatever is noble,
whatever is right,
whatever is pure,
whatever is lovely,
whatever is admirable—
if anything is excellent
or praiseworthy—
think about such things.

Philippians 4:8 NIV

He who sacrifices
thank offerings honors me,
and he prepares the way
so that I may show him
the salvation of God.

Thank God

PSALM 50:23
NIV

Let's be honest. During certain seasons of our lives, our circumstances
are such that we can be hard-pressed to find anything to be thankful for.
When you lose your job. When you lose someone you love.
When you lose your health. When you lose a dream...security...hope.
Life here on earth is full of losses that can leave you tongue-tied
when it comes to giving thanks.

But in those moments, more than in any others, thanksgiving
will be your strength as you praise God for who He is,
as you place your confidence in His provision and His promises for your life.

According to Psalm 50:23, in our times of trouble, thanksgiving that rises
despite our circumstances and emotions is not impossible.
It is, however, a choice. It is a decision we make in obedience to God's Word
and according to His will for our lives,
and it is a decision that honors God and moves His heart.
Somehow, when we offer up these bittersweet sacrifices to God,
a door in the heavenly realms opens, and our thanksgiving
prepares the way for God to reveal Himself to us in a new and powerful way.

God is honored when I give Him thanks during trials and tribulations
because with my thanksgiving I acknowledge Him as the Lord of my life...
the Lover of my soul...in both good times and bad.
Knowing that my sacrifices of thanksgiving open a door for God to move
on my behalf encourages my heart and gives me hope—
and that is truly something to be thankful for!

believe

The very first Bible study I was ever involved in focused on prayer.
The study was written for women, and in the section on thanksgiving,
the author suggested that we give thanks daily for our husbands.
Now I was a brand-new believer
and not used to giving thanks for much of anything...
especially not for my husband. But I wanted so much to please the Lord
that I went home that day, knelt by my bed, and asked God to show me
what about my husband I could be thankful for.

●　●　●

At first I thanked God for what I called the "positives of the negatives."
Thank You, Lord, that Michael doesn't do this and doesn't do that.
After a few days my prayers began to change.
Thank You, Lord, that Michael mows the grass and cuts the firewood.
Thank You, Jesus, that Michael gets up every morning and goes to work
even when he doesn't feel like it.
And Thank You, Lord, for my husband's adventurous spirit.
Our family has experienced many great adventures because of him!

As the days and weeks went on, an amazing thing happened.
I actually became thankful for my husband,
and my attitude toward him began to change.
Then, after a few more weeks, an even more amazing thing happened.
His attitude toward me began to change.

●　●　●

Within about six months from the time I began to give thanks for my husband—
and I did so purely out of obedience...despite my circumstances and emotions—
we began to see the salvation of the Lord in our marriage. It would be another
eighteen years before Michael accepted Christ for himself, but that attitude of
gratitude laid a foundation of faith that gave me hope in the waiting.

Heavenly Father,

Thank You for the Bible and how, through the written words You penned by Your Spirit, You have made not only Yourself known to me but also...

Your love for me through Jesus, the Living Word

Your heart, thoughts, and plans for man

Your truth that sets me free from the lies of self, Satan, and the world

Your comfort and encouragement that give me peace and confidence

Your precepts that train my heart to follow You

Your commands that teach me Your will and ways

Your statutes that counsel me and give me strength

Your promises that build my faith and fill me with hope

Your precepts that renew my mind and transform my life

Your joy that is made complete in me as I walk with You

Thank You, Father!

Where do you need to see the salvation of God in your life?
Begin today to offer up sacrifices of thanksgiving and see how God
wants to reveal Himself to you, in you, and through you...for His glory.

fashioned

I will praise you

for I am fearfully
and wonderfully made;

marvelous

are Your works!

Psalm 139:14

Sometimes when we count our blessings, we think only about what God has done for us or about what He has provided us. So I wonder when the last time was that you stopped to thank Him for how He created you.

Did I see you cringe? I know some of you were thinking, There isn't anything about me to give thanks for. And some of you are thinking it would be boastful to thank God for who you are.
Aren't we supposed to be humble?

Being a person who has spent most of her life feeling ashamed of who she is, I know now that God is pleased when we acknowledge that we are who we are by His divine design and His glorious grace.

I didn't create myself. Oh, I enjoy being creative, but the intricate design of a human being is far beyond my comprehension. But I can imagine that if I had created man in my image, I would hope he'd be grateful for the attributes that I built into him so he could enjoy life. I would hope that he would not take for granted his ability to see, smell, taste, touch, and hear.

As you think about the pleasure your five senses bring you, take a moment to stop and give God thanks for creating you just the way you are.

Delicious! Yummy! Scrumptious! Flavorful! Sweet! Savory! Tasty!

What would life be without these delightfully descriptive words
and the foods that evoke such language?
God designed our bodies to need food and the nutrients
that sustain good health...
but He also tucked little taste buds inside our mouths
so we could enjoy the flavors He created!
How dull and boring food would be without the gift of taste!

Many of us say grace before we eat. We give thanks to God
for His provision of food for our bodies, and that's a good thing.
But I wonder when you last thanked God
for the particular foods and flavors He's created to please your palate
or for the gift of taste buds so you can enjoy them.

We were not only created with a hunger and thirst
for good food and drink,
but also with a hunger and thirst for the good things of the Lord.

By choosing and delighting in God's ways and in His Word,
we are able, through faith, to taste His goodness and His glory.

Every morsel of love and grace,
every bite of His truth and drink of His Spirit,
is sweet to the palate of the soul
and nourishing to the spirit.

Give thanks to God for the gift of taste...
earthly as well as heavenly...
and for the food and drink that satisfy
our hunger and thirst for both.

43

Easy Harvest Home Cupcakes

1 box of carrot cake mix
1 cup walnuts

2 cups peeled chopped apples
3/4 cup flaked coconut

Prepare the cake mix according to the package directions and fold in the chopped apples. Fill paper-lined cupcake tins three-quarters full. Bake at 350° for 20 minutes or until a toothpick comes out clean. Cool and frost with Creamy Caramel Frosting. Makes about 20 cupcakes.

Creamy Caramel Frosting

2 tablespoons butter
3 tablespoons milk

1 cup powdered sugar, divided
1/2 teaspoon vanilla extract

1/2 cup firmly packed brown sugar

Melt the butter in a saucepan over medium heat. Stir in the milk and brown sugar. Boil vigorously for 1 minute. Remove from heat and beat in 1/2 cup of the powdered sugar. Cool about 5 minutes. Then beat in the vanilla and the remaining powdered sugar. Add more milk if necessary to make the frosting a good spreading consistency.

God's desire that we fully experience the world around us
is evident in the way He created us.

To breathe in the heavy fragrance of a rose can be intoxicating.
To inhale the salty ocean breeze can calm the soul.
And the aroma of freshly baked cookies can be so warm and inviting.

Even smells that make your nose curl can be a good thing.
Your baby's dirty diaper helps you know it's time for a change.
The smell of rotten eggs in the house warns you of a leaky gas line.
And that disgusting odor from the fridge is just saying, "It's time to clean!"

The earth is full of smells, and so are the heavenly realms.
God apparently loves a good aroma as much as we do.
The Bible tells us in Ephesians 5:2 that the sacrifice of Christ for our sins
is like sweet perfume to God...the fragrance of pure love.

As we give ourselves generously to love others the way Jesus loves us,
we also become a sweet-smelling fragrance to God.

Have you ever thanked God
for the aromas in your life and for your ability to smell them?
Have you thanked Him lately for the aroma of Christ?
There's no better time than right now to savor the fragrance
of His love and His blessings...and to give Him thanks!

Fragrant

We are
to God
the
Aroma
of Christ.

2 Corinthians 2:15

Blessed

God has so many wonderful things to show us,
but I wonder how many of these things we miss because we forget to look.

From the stately beauty of the oak tree to the intricate veining of its leaves,
we behold the beauty not only of creation but, more importantly, of its Creator!
Creation is a reflection of the heart of the Creator.
When you gaze at the star-filled sky, you're looking at the handiwork of God.
The infinite variety of colors in nature reveals the infinite nature of the Lord.
Birds, blossoms, bees, bunnies, babies...all God's creations.
That person next to you...yep...God's design.

Take a few minutes to pay attention to the amazing world around you, and
you will be awestruck by the glory of its design and its even more glorious Designer.

But God did not only give us earthly eyes; He also gave us spiritual eyes.
He longs for us to "fix our eyes on Jesus."
Even though we can't see God in the flesh, we can see Him through eyes of faith.
He revealed Himself to us through Jesus, and the better we know Jesus
and the more we trust Him, the more easily we are able to see Him at work
in our hearts and our circumstances and our world!

And as incredible as this beauty here on earth is, it is only a hint of the beauty
that awaits us in heaven when we will see the Lord Jesus face-to-face...
beholding Him in all His glory!

Give thanks today for the gift of sight and the beauty of God's creation!

Heavenly Father,
It's hard for me to imagine that You knew me even before I was born!
Whenever I read in Psalm 139 that You formed my inward parts
and knit me together in my mother's womb,
I am in awe of both Your love for me and Your incredible creativity!
Some say I was formed by chance...a random series of changes over time...
but the intricacy of how my body is woven together
testifies to a Creator and His divine design!

Even though I often take my body for granted, Lord,
today I am so thankful that You created me just the way I am.
I'm especially grateful that You gave me eyes to see the world around me—
both its beauty and its barrenness...
to be able to read my Bible and find You there in all Your glory...
to look into the eyes of the ones I love and recognize how truly special they are...
to be aware of the needs of those people You want me to reach out to...
and to notice the hurts of those You want me to comfort and encourage.

Thank You, Lord, for all the times You have allowed me to see myself
and my circumstances through Your eyes and not just my own.

Thank You for spiritual vision...
for the faith to look beyond the earthly to the eternal.

And, most of all, thank You for allowing me to behold Your beauty
and majesty in the everyday, ordinary moments of my life. Amen.

BLESSED are the PURE in heart for they shall see GOD.

Matthew 5:8

51

1. Come, ye thank-ful peo-ple, come— Raise the song of har-vest-home:
2. All the world is God's own field, Fruit un-to His praise to yield:
3. For the Lord our God shall come And shall take His har-vest home
4. E - ven so, Lord, quick-ly come To Thy fi - nal har-vest-home:

—Raise the song of har-vest
Wholesome grain and pure may
In His gar-ner ev-er-more
Raise the glo-rious har-vest-home

52

I like quiet. I enjoy peaceful places and the sound of birds singing.
But I also love the hearty laughter of my grandchildren playing,
and loud music energizes me to do my housework!

I am so thankful for the gift of hearing, yet how often I either take it for granted
or complain when the sounds I hear are not to my taste or timing.
It's funny how construction noises at my house don't seem to bother me
nearly as much as the same noises do when they're coming
from a neighbor's house!

There will always be sounds we want to listen to,
sounds like our favorite music, laughter, a baby's cooing, or a good conversation.
And there will be sounds that will—or should—cause us to cover our ears:
gossip, jackhammers, lies, fingernails screeching on a blackboard.
But aren't we glad we have ears to hear? I know I am!

When you read the Bible, you'll hear a lot of sounds.
You'll hear the cries and longings of people like you and me.
You'll hear the quiet whispers of God comforting the hearts of the tender
and His powerful truths giving guidance to the lost.
You'll hear strong commands empowering us to fight off evil
as well as triumphant shouts of victory and songs of celebration!

And you'll hear worship...songs of praise and thanksgiving...
from God's people down through the ages.
Can you hear them? Lift your voice and join the chorus.
Give God thanks! It will be music to His ears!

Have you ever walked through a fabric store or clothing store
and just enjoyed touching...sometimes even fondling...
the various textures along the way? How about in the baby department?
Could you resist caressing those soft cuddly flannels and fleeces?

Texture adds spice to life, punch to decorating,
pizzazz to food, and flavor to art.
But what value would tactile texture have if God had not designed us with
nerve endings that enable us to feel and enjoy the sensation?
Sometimes I think we underestimate the power of touch, especially hugging,
as a vitally important expression of caring for one another.

What's amazing to me is the power we have to touch people
and be touched by people without physical contact.
A compliment, an encouraging card in the mail, or an act of kindness,
such as a meal during a time of need or a word of correction spoken in love,
can sometimes touch a person's heart in a way that even a hug cannot.

This kind of emotional texture stirs a heart to thanksgiving...
to know that someone cares enough to express love in a meaningful way.
And it's this kind of touch that God uses to reveal Himself to us.
He touches our hearts with His love,
He touches our minds with His truth, and
He touches our lives with His transforming power.

Thank You, God, for the gift of touch!

heart

hugs

Let the words of my mouth
and the meditation of my heart
be acceptable in Your sight,
O LORD, my strength
and my redeemer.

Psalm 19:14

As you consider the fives senses God has given you—
sight, sound, touch, taste, and smell—
express below your gratefulness to Him for the things that come to mind.

Every good and perfect gift is from above.

James 1:17 NIV

to:
from: God

Not all gifts are given for the right reasons, are they?
A gift is to be an expression of love, but sometimes we give out of obligation.
Gifts are to be given to bless, but sometimes we give them to impress, don't we?

Not so with God!
God is love, and every gift He gives is a perfect expression of His loving nature.
He doesn't bless you out of duty. He blesses you because He wants to.
He loves you and showers you with gifts of every kind.
Spiritual. Physical. Material. Mental. Emotional. Relational.
If you were to write a list of God's blessings, it would truly be never ending
for every breath you take...every moment of your life is a gift!

You've heard it before:
Your life is God's gift to you, and what you do with it is your gift back to God.
We can sing our praises to the Lord.
We can whisper our gratitude in the quietness of our prayers.
We can clap our hands and dance with joy.
But one expression of thanksgiving rises above all the rest.
It's obedience.
Jesus said the greatest commands are these:
Love the Lord your God with all your heart, mind, soul, and strength.
Love your neighbor as yourself.

Giving thanks is not only expressed in words but also in deeds.
God has given you this incredible gift of life, and the one thing He asks
is that you give it away...by loving others as He loves you...
and to do so with a thankful heart.

Blessed be the Lord,
who daily loads us
with benefits,
the God
of our salvation.

Psalm 68:19

Bless the LORD, O my soul,
and forget not all His benefits.

Psalm 103:2

Living in a world of information overload, we can easily forget things...where we put the keys, what time that appointment is, what I ate for breakfast just this morning! At times, I've even forgotten the names of people that I know well!

But nothing can affect how we live our lives more than forgetting the benefits of the Lord! When we forget what God has done for us in the past, we lose hope for the future and become discouraged. However, when we remind ourselves of how God has saved our souls, answered our prayers, and met our needs, our faith is renewed and our hearts overflow with thanksgiving!

Keeping a Thanksgiving Journal is a great way to not forget God's blessings, as well as increase your awareness of His presence in your life. Take a moment at the end of every day to recall and note just how beautiful that sunset was, how grateful you are for running water, or how God answered a particular prayer. I guarantee that once you start looking for things to be thankful for, the more thankful you'll become!

Try it. It might just change how you see your life!

We were created for relationship...with God and with others.
Our lives are filled with a variety of people whom God uses to fill our cups
and bless our lives. Some we know well; some we barely know at all.
We have family, friends, and neighbors. We have pastors, doctors, and dentists.
We depend on bank tellers, mail carriers, and grocery store clerks.
We labor together with our co-workers on the job and in ministry.
And of course we can't forget the teachers, coaches, and other parents
who play such a big part in the growth of our children.

The list could go on and on to include everyone from the person
who picked the tea leaves so you could savor the flavor of your favorite brew...
to the factory worker who painted the design on your pretty teacup.

It's so easy to take people for granted, isn't it?
Especially the ones who mean the most to you!
So take some time today to stop and thank God for the people in your life and,
as a blessing to God, look for ways in the coming days to say "thank you" to them.

But remember...not even the people we love and those who love us
can ever fill our deepest relational needs.
Our cups can only overflow when Jesus is our very Best Friend of all.
He knows us better than anyone else, and He loves us more than anyone else loves us.
He gave His life for us, and He alone is the perfect Friend.

Now that's something to be thankful for!

Give thanks
with a
grateful
heart

Autumn Spice Pumpkin Bread

1 15-oz can pumpkin puree
4 eggs
1 cup vegetable oil
2/3 cup water
3 cups white sugar

3 cups flour
2 tsp baking soda
1 1/2 tsp salt
1 tsp ground cinnamon
1 tsp ground nutmeg
1/2 tsp ground cloves
1/2 tsp ground ginger
1 cup chopped walnuts
1 cup dried cranberries

Great for gift giving

1. Preheat oven to 350°. Grease and flour three 7x3-inch loaf pans or six 3x5-inch pans.
2. In a large bowl, mix pumpkin puree, eggs, oil, water, and sugar until well blended.
3. In a separate bowl, whisk together the flour, baking soda, salt, cinnamon, nutmeg, cloves, and ginger.
4. Stir the dry ingredients into the pumpkin mixture until just blended. Add the walnuts and cranberries. Pour into prepared pans.
5. Bake 7x3 loaves about 50 minutes or 3x5 loaves for about 30 minutes. Loaves are done when a toothpick comes out clean!

I can still remember those first few months back in the Mainland after we'd lived four years in rural Alaska. I especially recall the smile that crossed my face and the gratitude that welled up in my heart every time I turned on the faucet!
Not only did water come out, but the water was hot! I smile now just thinking about it!

You see, for three years we did not have indoor plumbing. We hauled the water we needed for cooking and cleaning up in five-gallon cans and heated it on the stove. Our outhouse was about a thirty-foot walk from the back door, which seemed like a mile at thirty degrees below zero! And the local store was the place to go for weekly showers, laundry, and catching up on all the latest area news.

For us, moving to Alaska had been a lifestyle choice.
And as difficult as life there was, compared to many other parts of the world, we were blessed beyond measure and grateful for what we did have.

I wonder if you are grateful for what you have, or are you disgruntled, caught in the cultural clutches of always wanting more and better?

Let me ask a few questions. When you turn on the faucet, does water flow?
When you flip the switch, do the lights come on?
Do you have food in your cupboard and a stove to cook it on...
a bed to sleep in and a closet in which to hang your clothes?

These are all creature comforts that most of the world does not enjoy.
Can you imagine living without them? Think about it.
Then ask God to forgive you for taking so much for granted—
and give Him thanks for the abundant blessings that are yours today!

67

Like many people, I can even take church for granted.
I'm not talking so much about the structure or the service
as much as the fact that we, as believers in the Lord Jesus Christ,
can gather together to worship Him, learn about Him, and talk about Him
without fear of being arrested, imprisoned, or killed.

We can buy Bibles and read them openly in public.
We can wear Jesus T-shirts and put Jesus bumper stickers on our cars.
We can play music about God in our cars even with the windows rolled down.
Not everyone will agree with us or like us for it,
but right now, at this point in our history,
we are not afraid to do these things.

I am thankful that we live in a nation where we have this freedom,
but I don't think about it often enough. I most often just take for granted this
freedom to worship when it's actually a privilege we've been given.

Even more than that, I am thankful we have the freedom to love one another.
Do we always walk in this freedom? No, but hopefully we're growing in it.
And that's a freedom no one can take away from us.

Jesus came to set the captives free, and when He did,
He opened our hearts, filled them with His love, and sealed them
with the Holy Spirit. He now lives in us and through us.
Now that's genuine freedom...and that's something to GIVE THANKS for!

Caramel Apples

6 to 8 apples   1-pound bag of caramels
2 tablespoons milk   Wooden sticks or sturdy twigs
Butter (1 stick)   Wax paper
Chopped walnuts, mini-chocolate chips, or sprinkles of your choice

1. Dip apples briefly in boiling water to remove any wax that might keep the caramel from sticking to the apples. Remove the stems, dry the apples, and cool them in the refrigerator for about 10 minutes.

2. Line a cookie sheet with buttered wax paper.

3. Insert one stick into each apple where its stem was.

4. Pour the nuts, the chocolate chips, and/or the sprinkles into separate shallow bowls.

5. Place caramel and milk in a deep microwavable bowl. Microwave at full power for 1 minute and stir. Microwave for 30 more seconds and then stir until caramel is completely melted.

6. Dip the chilled apples into the caramel and then into the toppings.

7. Set the caramel apples on wax paper to cool.

to:

To be an autumn blessing to a family you know, consider giving them a bag of apples along with the caramels, some sticks, and this recipe. Include a note telling them how thankful you are for them and let them know that they are the apple of God's eye!

An attitude of gratitude
will chase the blues away.
Consider all God's given you
and let Him hear you say—

Thank You, Father, for this moment,
open my eyes that I may see,
forgive me for all I take for granted—
Your love and blessings that flow so free.

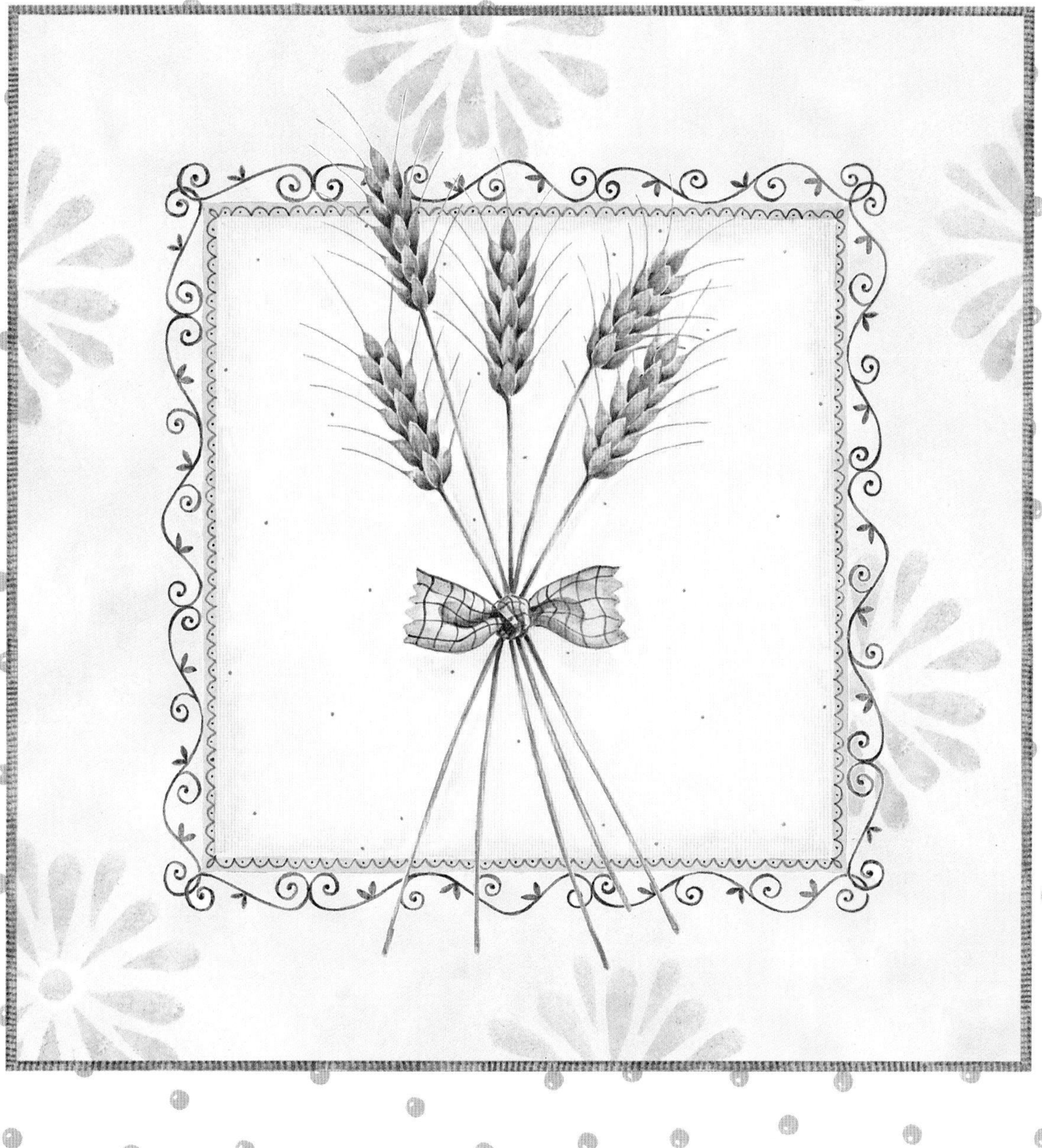

You may not know what your tomorrows hold, but as a believer in Christ Jesus,
you know the One who does. And He has a perfect plan for your life.
He doesn't want you to waste precious time today worrying about tomorrow...
about things you have no control over or situations that will never come to pass.
Instead Jesus wants you to trust Him and to give Him thanks today
for what He has blessed you with presently
as well as for what He has in store for you tomorrow. Yes. Sight unseen.
That kind of thanksgiving is called faith.

The Lord has given you very great and wonderful promises concerning your future.
He assures you that His plan for you is to bless you and not to harm you.
Life will not be pain-free, but it will be perfect for who you are
and for where God wants to take you. And as you walk with Him, He will faithfully
reveal His plan to you one step at a time.

So begin right now...wherever you are emotionally, physically, spiritually...
to give God thanks. As you do, I guarantee your hope will increase,
your future will begin to look brighter, and you might even begin to sense
a glimmer of joyful expectation, wondering what God will do next.

None of us knows what the future holds, but because we know the One who holds
the future, we can face our tomorrows with confidence.

And hope does not disappoint us, because God has poured out
his love into our hearts by the Holy Spirit, whom he has given us.
Romans 5:5 NIV

"I know the plans
I have for you,"
declares the LORD,
"plans to prosper you
and not to harm you,
plans to give you
hope and a future."

Jeremiah 29:11 NIV

When you think about how God's plan for your life...
past, present, and future...what are you most thankful for?

_____

_____

_____

_____

_____

_____

_____

_____

_____

_____

_____

_____

Dear Friend,

Thank you, once again, for allowing me to share my heart with you through my art and stories. Creating this book has brought me great joy!

God's timing for me to write and illustrate "Give Thanks" could not have been better, as I've experienced some difficult days during its creation, including my mother passing away. But it is during the most trying times in life, when our hearts are laid open and we are the most vulnerable, that a grateful heart becomes our strength and song to carry on. I hope you will find the same is true for you.

Life is short for all of us, and how we live it is by our choice. My hope is that you are choosing to live your life in relationship with Jesus Christ. He loves you so much that He died on the cross so your sins could be forgiven. But He didn't stay in the grave. He resurrected so you could have a new life...a life overflowing with love and gratitude.

The Bible tells us Jesus stands at the door of our heart and knocks (Revelation 3:20). He won't come in unless you hand Him the key and invite Him to enter in. If you've never done this, will you open the door to Him today? Remember...He invites us to come just as we are. So ask Him to be your Savior, to forgive your sins, and to fill you with His love. And He will! Now that is something to be thankful for!

I thank God for you...in His love, and always for His glory!
Karla

If God has used this book to encourage your heart or help you in your walk with Christ, I'd like to hear from you! Please write me at:

Karla Dornacher
P.O. Box 185
Battle Ground, WA 98604

Or email me at:
karla@karladornacher.com

For more information regarding my other books or speaking ministry, please email me or visit:
www.karladornacher.com

For a glimpse into my daily life, contests, and more, please visit:
http://www.karladornacher.typepad.com/.